ONE-POT
5-INGREDIENTS
WONDER

GARDEN of GRAPES.

First Edition: 2023

Published by Garden of Grapes.

Printed in USA

The recipes, techniques, and tips in this cookbook are intended for personal use only. The author and publisher are not responsible for any adverse effects or consequences resulting from the use of the recipes or suggestions in this book.

Library of Congress Cataloging-in-Publication Data:

First edition.
Includes index.

Manufactured in USA

Introduction

Ladies, gentlemen, and passionate cooks,

Welcome to the world of culinary convenience, a realm where the art of gastronomy finds its place in the simplest of kitchens. As you turn the pages of the "One-Pot 5-Ingredient Wonders" cookbook, I extend to you a warm and hearty greeting. Whether you're a seasoned home chef or just getting your feet wet in the vast sea of cooking, you've picked up a treasure trove of culinary wisdom.

Cooking, in all its glory, is not just about creating dishes; it's an exploration of tastes, a journey of ingredients, and a testament to the beauty of simplicity. In this cookbook, we delve into the magic that unfolds when you combine the finest of ingredients in a single pot.

The inspiration for this collection of recipes stems from countless moments of revelation in the kitchen. You see, I've traveled the world, tasted its diverse flavors, and had the privilege of enjoying the creations of both grandmothers and world-renowned chefs. Through all these experiences, I realized that delicious food need not be complicated.

The recipes within these pages have been carefully crafted to bring the essence of various cuisines to your home, making you feel like a culinary virtuoso with minimal effort. We'll uncover the secrets behind one-pot wonders that not only simplify your time in the kitchen but also elevate your dining experience.

What can you expect to find in this culinary trove, you ask? Well, anticipate a symphony of flavors, all harmonizing effortlessly within one pot. There will be rich stews, aromatic curries, soul-soothing soups, and delightful pasta dishes. These recipes celebrate the very essence of cooking - creating hearty, mouthwatering dishes with the least amount of hassle.

Whether you're a busy parent, a working professional, or someone who just craves simplicity in the kitchen, this cookbook has something for you. Expect vibrant photos that will tantalize your taste buds, easy-to-follow instructions that will keep you confident in the kitchen, and a culinary journey that will transport you around the world from the comfort of your home.

So, as we embark on this adventure together, remember that the heart of any meal is the passion you infuse into it. Cooking is an art, but it's also a way to spread love, share memories, and create moments that linger on the taste buds and in the soul.

Get ready to wield your spatula and stir your imagination. The "One-Pot 5-Ingredient Wonders" cookbook is your passport to a simpler, more delectable way of cooking. Bon appétit!

Yours in culinary exploration,
Garden of Grapes

Creamy Alfredo Fettuccine
See page, 14

Cooking Philosophy or Approach

One-Pot 5-Ingredient Wonders: Where Culinary Magic Happens in a Single Pot

Allow me to take you on a journey into the heart of my culinary philosophy and the very essence of the "One-Pot 5-Ingredient Wonders" cookbook. This isn't just a collection of recipes; it's a testament to my approach to food, cooking, and the joy of creating simple yet exceptional dishes.

At its core, my approach is all about embracing the beauty of minimalism in cooking. With just one pot and five ingredients, we strip away the complexities and get back to what really matters: the pure flavors of the ingredients themselves. It's a celebration of how a handful of elements, carefully chosen and thoughtfully combined, can create dishes that are not only delicious but also a breeze to prepare.

Technique-wise, it's all about efficiency and maximizing flavor. We want those five ingredients to shine, and that means employing techniques that extract every bit of potential. Whether it's searing to create a caramelized crust on a succulent piece of meat, simmering to infuse a broth with deep flavors, or a simple sauté to coax out the best from vegetables, every step is a deliberate choice to elevate the final dish.

Now, about the ingredients themselves. Quality, not quantity, is the name of the game. It's about using the very best, freshest ingredients we can find. I'm talking about vibrant produce, ethically raised meats, and flavorful seasonings. We let these ingredients speak for themselves, and that's where the magic lies.

What defines the recipes in this cookbook is the way they showcase the harmony between these elements. The recipes are a testament to simplicity, but they're far from ordinary. They're about coaxing out bold, robust, and complex flavors from just a handful of components. It's a testament to the power of restraint in cooking.

In this culinary journey, I encourage you to let go of the notion that great food must be complicated or time-consuming. We've distilled the essence of gourmet cooking into straightforward, easy-to-follow recipes that prove that sometimes, less is indeed more.

It's about enjoying the culinary experience without the stress, savoring every bite, and sharing fantastic meals with loved ones. This cookbook isn't just a collection of recipes; it's an invitation to a simpler, more joyful way of cooking. I hope you find as much pleasure in preparing and savoring these One-Pot 5-Ingredient Wonders as I did in creating them.

Cheers to culinary excellence in its purest and most simplified form,
Garden of Grapes

Tips for Successful Cooking

Ladies and gentlemen, home cooks and culinary adventurers,

As we delve into the world of "One-Pot 5-Ingredient Wonders," we're about to embark on a gastronomic journey, and I want to ensure that your path is as smooth as silk and as flavorful as it gets. Here's a glimpse of some valuable tips and tricks that will guide you to success in your one-pot cooking endeavors.

1. The Right Pot Matters: First and foremost, the choice of your one-pot vessel is crucial. Ensure it's sturdy, well-sized for your recipe, and has a tight-fitting lid. This is your trusty companion on this culinary adventure, so choose wisely.

2. Prepping Like a Pro: Before you even think about the stove, have everything ready. This means washing, chopping, and measuring your ingredients. We're aiming for simplicity, and that means no mid-cooking rushes to the pantry.

3. Building Flavor Layers: Great one-pot dishes are all about flavor. Start by searing your proteins to develop a rich base. Then, sauté your aromatics (like onions and garlic) to build complexity. And if your recipe includes spices, blooming them in oil can make a huge flavor difference.

4. Timing is Everything: Different ingredients take different times to cook. Add the ingredients that need the most time first, and the quicker-cooking ones later. Don't rush, let the magic happen gradually.

5. Control the Heat: One-pot cooking is like conducting an orchestra. Adjust the heat as you go to keep everything in harmony. Sometimes a rolling boil, sometimes a gentle simmer - you're the maestro.

6. Lid On, Lid Off: The lid is your secret weapon. It traps steam and helps ingredients cook evenly. But don't forget to remove it occasionally to reduce and thicken sauces or soups.

7. Taste as You Go: The best chefs always taste their food as they cook. Adjust the seasoning as needed. Remember, you're the boss of your pot!

8. Don't Peek Too Often: Every time you lift that lid, you're letting out precious heat and moisture. Keep it on, and let the flavors meld and mingle.

9. Patience is a Virtue: Good things come to those who wait. Let your one-pot dish rest for a bit before digging in. This allows the flavors to meld and intensify.

10. Enjoy the Journey: One-pot cooking is an art that's meant to be savored. Take your time, enjoy the process, and embrace the wonderful scents that will fill your kitchen.

With these tips in your culinary arsenal, you're well on your way to becoming a one-pot wonder. Whether it's a hearty stew, a fragrant curry, or a delightful pasta dish, may your one-pot creations be nothing short of miraculous. Remember, cooking is an adventure, and you're the intrepid explorer. Bon appétit!

Kitchen Essentials

Kitchen Essentials

Ah, the dance of the kitchen, where magic and deliciousness unfold. To create the culinary wonders we've shared in this book, you'll need a few trusty tools and gadgets. Consider these your kitchen sidekicks on the path to culinary excellence. Here's a rundown of the essential kitchen tools and equipment that will often make an appearance in our recipes:

1. Chef's Knife: Your faithful companion in the kitchen, capable of slicing, dicing, chopping, and mincing with grace. Invest in a good quality chef's knife; it's your partner in crime.

2. Cutting Board: To give your knife a stable surface to work on. Wooden or plastic, it's your choice, but make sure it's spacious enough.

3. Pots and Pans: A reliable set of pots and pans in various sizes. You'll find yourself reaching for them frequently to simmer, sauté, and sear.

4. Cast Iron Skillet: The workhorse of the kitchen, capable of going from stovetop to oven. It's perfect for dishes that need that extra searing or caramelization.

5. Baking Sheets: Ideal for roasting vegetables, baking cookies, or crisping up some appetizers.

6. Spatula: You'll be flipping, scraping, and stirring with this handy tool.

7. Tongs: Perfect for handling hot foods, grilling, or even serving.

8. Measuring Cups and Spoons: For precision in your recipes.

9. Grater/Zester: Whether it's cheese, lemon zest, or fresh nutmeg, a grater is a versatile tool.

10. Mixing Bowls: In various sizes, because the kitchen is all about mixing it up.

11. Whisk: For beating eggs, making dressings, and ensuring a lump-free sauce.

12. Can Opener: For those recipes that call for canned ingredients.

13. Colander/Strainer: To drain pasta, rice, and to rinse fruits and veggies.

14. Kitchen Timer: To keep your culinary creations from turning into fiery disasters.

15. Blender/Food Processor: For smoothies, soups, sauces, and purees.

16. Oven: The heart of your kitchen where roasting, baking, and broiling happen.

17. Microwave: When you need things done in a flash.

Tips on How to Use These Tools Effectively

- Knife Skills: A sharp knife is safer and more effective. Keep your knives honed and learn proper cutting techniques to make your prep work a breeze.

- Heat Control: Get to know your stovetop. Different dishes require different levels of heat. Low and slow for simmering, high for searing.

- Season Your Pans: Seasoning a cast-iron skillet is like giving it armor. It prevents sticking and keeps your skillet in top shape. Rub it with oil and bake it empty for an hour at 375°F.

- Proper Measuring: For dry ingredients, level off the measuring cups and spoons. For liquids, use a clear measuring cup and check at eye level for accuracy.

- Cleaning and Care: Keep your tools clean and dry. Wooden tools can crack or warp if left in water. Non-stick pans need gentle treatment to keep their coating intact.

- Patience with Heat: When cooking meat, give it time to rest after cooking. This lets the juices redistribute for a juicier result.

- Preheat the Oven: When baking, make sure your oven is properly preheated before sliding anything inside. This ensures even cooking.

So, there you have it, the arsenal of kitchen tools and some handy tips to wield them like a culinary pro. In your culinary journey, they'll become trusted allies, turning your one-pot creations into culinary masterpieces.

One-Pot Goulash
See page, 20

Flavor Pairing Suggestions

One-Pot 5-Ingredient Wonders: Culinary Creativity in a Single Pot

Ah, the wonders of culinary exploration, where the boundaries of flavor are only limited by your imagination. In this culinary journey of 'One-Pot 5-Ingredient Wonders,' you've already discovered the joys of simplicity, time-efficiency, and downright deliciousness. But what if we told you that this is just the beginning?

Flavor Pairing Suggestions:

Indeed, it's time to don your chef's hat, or perhaps your mad scientist's lab coat, because we're diving into the realm of flavor pairing suggestions. This section is where the magic happens. It's where you transform your already fantastic one-pot recipes into your own culinary masterpieces.

Imagine your pot as a canvas, and your ingredients as the colors on your palette. Now, with a dash of creativity, a pinch of boldness, and perhaps a sprinkle of audacity, you can create a symphony of flavors that'll dance across your taste buds. Here are some ideas to get your creative juices flowing:

1. **Citrus Zest and Fresh Herbs:** A simple addition of lemon or orange zest and a handful of fresh basil, mint, or cilantro can brighten up your one-pot dishes. Try it with chicken, pasta, or seafood for a burst of freshness.

2. **Spice It Up:** A pinch of chili flakes, cayenne, or a dash of your favorite hot sauce can give your dishes a fiery kick. Experiment with your spice tolerance, and see how it transforms the flavors.

3. **Nuts and Seeds:** Toasted almonds, pine nuts, sesame seeds, or pumpkin seeds add a lovely crunch and nuttiness to your one-pot meals. Sprinkle them over rice, couscous, or vegetable dishes for extra texture.

4. **Cheese, Please:** A sprinkle of grated Parmesan, crumbled feta, or creamy goat cheese can elevate your pasta and grain-based recipes to new heights of savory delight.

5. Balsamic Reduction: A drizzle of balsamic reduction over roasted or grilled meats can provide a delightful sweet and tangy contrast.

6. Sweet with Savory: Experiment with adding a small amount of honey, maple syrup, or a fruit preserve to balance savory dishes. Try it in your braised meat or roasted vegetable recipes.

7. Freshness of Greens: A handful of arugula, spinach, or kale stirred into your warm one-pot creations just before serving adds a touch of freshness and color.

8. Caramelized Onion Magic: Slowly sautéed and deeply caramelized onions can be your secret weapon for extra depth of flavor in soups, stews, and risottos.

9. International Inspiration: Draw from the diverse world of cuisines. Consider adding coconut milk to your curry, soy sauce to stir-fry, or sumac to your roasted vegetables.

10. Sour Cream and Yogurt: A dollop of sour cream or Greek yogurt can bring creaminess and a hint of tang to your dishes. Use it with chili, goulash, or even creamy pasta.

Remember, dear culinary adventurers, the key to flavor pairing is experimentation. Don't be afraid to bend the rules and follow your taste buds. The beauty of these one-pot wonders lies in their adaptability and potential for endless creativity.

So, unleash your inner culinary artist, and let the symphony of flavors begin. Your one-pot creation might just become the next masterpiece in the world of gastronomy. Bon appétit, and happy experimenting!

Spicy Sausage and Rice
See page, 33

INDEX

Chapter 1:
Hearty Soups & Stews

4 servings

250 cal

20 min

Chicken and Rice Soup

A comforting classic with a twist! This soup brings warmth to your soul with tender chicken and aromatic rice, perfect for any day.

Ingredients:

- 1 lb chicken thighs
- 1 cup rice
- 2 carrots, diced
- 1 onion, chopped
- 4 cups chicken broth

Directions

1. Heat olive oil in a pot.
2. Sauté onions and carrots.
3. Add chicken, rice, and broth.
4. Simmer until chicken is cooked.
5. Serve and enjoy!

Fun Facts

Did you know? Chicken soup has been cherished for centuries as a natural remedy for colds and flu due to its soothing properties.

6
servings

350 cal

25 min

Beef and Vegetable Stew

A hearty medley of beef, veggies, and savory broth, this stew will fill your home with irresistible aromas.

Ingredients:

- 1 lb beef chunks
- 4 potatoes, cubed
- 2 carrots, sliced
- 1 onion, minced
- 4 cups beef broth

Directions

1. Brown beef in a pot.
2. Add veggies and broth.
3. Simmer until tender.
4. Serve with crusty bread!

Fun Facts

Did you know? Stews have been a favorite among travelers for centuries, as they're easy to prepare and transport.

4
servings

180 cal

30 min

Potato Leek Soup

Creamy and dreamy, this soup blends velvety potatoes and leeks, creating a rich, comforting bowl of goodness.

Ingredients:

- 4 large potatoes, peeled
- 3 leeks, sliced
- 4 cups vegetable broth
- 1/2 cup heavy cream

Directions

1. Sauté leeks in butter.
2. Add potatoes and broth.
3. Simmer until soft.
4. Blend until creamy.
5. Add cream, salt, and pepper.
6. Enjoy!

Fun Facts

Did you know? Leeks are a symbol of Wales and have been worn as emblems in the caps of Welsh soldiers for centuries.

5
servings

220 cal

35 min

Lentil and Carrot Stew

Packed with protein and flavor, this stew combines earthy lentils and sweet carrots for a hearty, nutritious meal.

Ingredients:

- 1 cup lentils
- 3 carrots, diced
- 1 onion, chopped
- 4 cups vegetable broth
- 2 tsp cumin

Directions

1. Sauté onions and carrots.
2. Add lentils, cumin, and broth.
3. Simmer until lentils are tender.
4. Serve hot.

Fun Facts

Did you know? Lentils are one of the oldest known food sources, dating back more than 9,000 years.

4
servings

190 cal

15 min

Easy

Tomato Basil Soup

A timeless favorite, this soup combines ripe tomatoes and fragrant basil for a burst of summer in every spoonful.

Ingredients:

- 6 ripe tomatoes, chopped
- 2 cups vegetable broth
- 1/2 cup fresh basil leaves
- 2 cloves garlic

Directions

1. Sauté garlic in olive oil.
2. Add tomatoes and broth.
3. Simmer until tomatoes soften.
4. Add basil, blend, and serve.

Fun Facts

Did you know? Tomatoes were once considered poisonous in Europe, but they are now a staple in countless dishes.

6
servings

280 cal

20 min

Minestrone Soup

A delightful Italian classic, this soup is a medley of vegetables, beans, and pasta, creating a satisfying and filling meal.

Ingredients:

- 1 cup pasta
- 2 zucchinis, diced
- 2 carrots, sliced
- 1 onion, minced
- 4 cups vegetable broth

Directions

1. Sauté onions, carrots, and zucchinis.
2. Add broth and pasta.
3. Simmer until pasta is tender.
4. Serve with grated cheese.

Fun Facts

Did you know? Minestrone soup varies across Italy, with each region adding its own unique ingredients and flavors.

4
servings

220 cal

30 min

Butternut Squash Bisque

Creamy and indulgent, this bisque showcases the sweet, nutty flavor of butternut squash, perfect for a cozy evening.

Ingredients:

- 1 butternut squash, peeled and cubed
- 1 onion, chopped
- 4 cups vegetable broth
- 1/2 cup cream

Directions

1. Sauté onions until translucent.
2. Add squash and broth.
3. Simmer until squash is soft.
4. Blend until smooth.
5. Stir in cream.
6. Enjoy!

Fun Facts

Did you know? Butternut squash was first cultivated in Central and South America over 7,000 years ago.

6
servings

320 cal

25 min

Spicy Chili

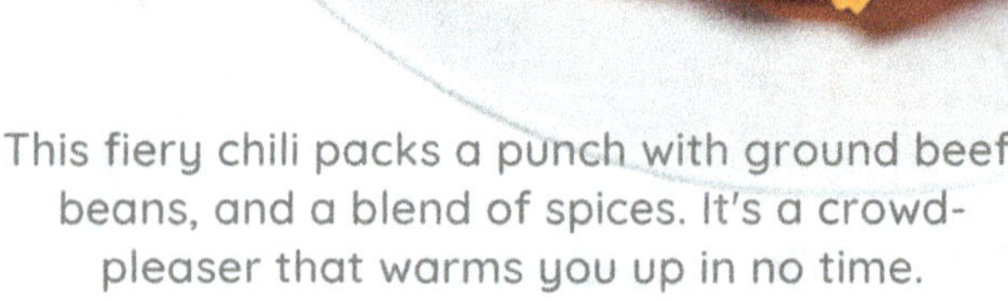

This fiery chili packs a punch with ground beef, beans, and a blend of spices. It's a crowd-pleaser that warms you up in no time.

Ingredients:

- 1 lb ground beef
- 2 cans kidney beans
- 1 onion, chopped
- 2 cloves garlic
- 2 cups tomato sauce

Directions

1. Brown beef with onions and garlic.
2. Add beans, tomato sauce, and spices.
3. Simmer for a spicy kick.
4. Serve with cheese and sour cream.

Fun Facts

Did you know? Chili con carne, a variant of chili, is the official state dish of Texas and has a rich history dating back to the 19th century.

4
servings

240 cal

20 min

Creamy Mushroom Soup

Luxuriously creamy and rich, this mushroom soup is a umami-packed delight. It's a culinary masterpiece with only five ingredients!

Ingredients:

- 1 lb mushrooms, sliced
- 1 onion, minced
- 4 cups chicken broth
- 1/2 cup heavy cream

Directions

1. Sauté mushrooms and onions until tender.
2. Add broth and simmer.
3. Blend until smooth.
4. Stir in cream.
5. Savor the magic!

Fun Facts

Did you know? Mushrooms are often called the "meat" of the vegetable world due to their savory, umami flavor.

4
servings

210 cal

15 min

Vegetable Noodle Soup

A light and refreshing soup that combines colorful vegetables and tender noodles. It's like a hug in a bowl!

Ingredients:

- 2 cups egg noodles
- 2 carrots, sliced
- 2 zucchinis, diced
- 4 cups vegetable broth

Directions

1. Cook noodles separately.
2. Sauté carrots and zucchinis.
3. Add broth and simmer.
4. Combine noodles and veggies.
5. Serve and enjoy!

Fun Facts

Did you know? Noodles are believed to have originated in China over 4,000 years ago and have since spread worldwide.

Chapter 2:
Pasta Pleasures

4
servings

320 cal

15 min

One-Pot Spaghetti Aglio e Olio

A timeless Italian classic that celebrates simplicity and flavor.

Ingredients:

- 12 oz spaghetti
- 4 cloves garlic, sliced
- 1/4 cup olive oil
- 1/2 tsp red pepper flakes

Directions

1. Cook spaghetti until al dente.
2. Sauté garlic and pepper flakes in olive oil.
3. Toss spaghetti in the garlic oil.
4. Garnish with parsley and Parmesan.

Fun Facts

Did you know? "Aglio e olio" means "garlic and oil" in Italian, highlighting the primary ingredients of this dish.

4
servings

380 cal

20 min

Creamy Alfredo Fettuccine

Indulge in the velvety richness of this classic Alfredo sauce.

Ingredients:

- 8 oz fettuccine
- 1/2 cup heavy cream
- 1/2 cup grated Parmesan
- 2 cloves garlic

Directions

1. Cook fettuccine until al dente.
2. Simmer cream and garlic until thickened.
3. Stir in Parmesan.
4. Toss with pasta and enjoy!

Fun Facts

Did you know? Alfredo sauce was created by a Roman restaurateur named Alfredo di Lelio in the early 20th century.

4
servings

330 cal

25 min

Lemon Garlic Shrimp Pasta

A zesty and refreshing pasta dish with succulent shrimp.

Ingredients:

- 8 oz spaghetti
- 1 lb shrimp, peeled
- 2 cloves garlic, minced
- Zest and juice of 1 lemon

Directions

1. Cook spaghetti until al dente.
2. Sauté shrimp and garlic until pink.
3. Add lemon zest and juice.
4. Toss with pasta and serve.

Fun Facts

Did you know? Shrimp is a rich source of vitamin B12, which is essential for maintaining healthy nerve cells.

4
servings

420 cal

30 min

Beef Stroganoff

A hearty and creamy Russian-inspired dish
that's a true crowd-pleaser.

Ingredients:

- 1 lb beef strips
- 1 onion, chopped
- 1/2 cup sour cream
- 2 tbsp Dijon mustard

Directions

1. Sauté beef and onions until browned.
2. Stir in sour cream and mustard.
3. Simmer until heated through.
4. Serve over cooked noodles.

Fun Facts

Did you know? Beef Stroganoff is named after
Count Pavel Stroganov, a 19th-century Russian
aristocrat and diplomat.

4
servings

280 cal

15 min

Tomato Basil Penne

Embrace the classic combination of ripe tomatoes and fragrant basil.

Ingredients:

- 8 oz penne pasta
- 4 ripe tomatoes, diced
- 1/2 cup fresh basil leaves
- 2 cloves garlic

Directions

1. Cook penne until al dente.
2. Sauté garlic and tomatoes until softened.
3. Add basil.
4. Toss with pasta and enjoy!

Fun Facts

Did you know? Basil is considered a symbol of love in Italy, and it's a common ingredient in Italian cuisine.

4
servings

340 cal

25 min

Spinach and Artichoke Mac and Cheese

A creamy mac and cheese with a delightful twist of spinach and artichokes.

Ingredients:

- 8 oz macaroni
- 2 cups shredded cheddar
- 1 cup chopped spinach
- 1 cup chopped artichoke hearts

Directions

1. Cook macaroni until al dente.
2. Mix in cheddar, spinach, and artichokes.
3. Stir until cheese melts.
4. Dive in!

Fun Facts

Did you know? Spinach is packed with iron, making it a fantastic choice for maintaining healthy blood.

4
servings

360 cal

20 min

Creamy Pesto Orzo

A luscious dish that combines the flavors of basil pesto and creamy orzo.

Ingredients:

- 1 cup orzo pasta
- 1/2 cup basil pesto
- 1/2 cup heavy cream
- 1/2 cup grated Parmesan

Directions

1. Cook orzo until al dente.
2. Stir in pesto, cream, and Parmesan.
3. Heat until creamy and delicious.
4. Serve and savor!

Fun Facts

Did you know? Pesto originated in Genoa, Italy, and its name comes from the Italian word "pestare," meaning "to pound."

6 servings

290 cal

30 min

One-Pot Goulash

A hearty Hungarian stew with tender beef and a paprika-infused sauce.

Ingredients:

- 1 lb beef stew meat
- 1 onion, chopped
- 2 red bell peppers, diced
- 2 tbsp paprika

Directions

1. Sauté beef and onions until browned.
2. Add peppers, paprika, and water.
3. Simmer until meat is tender.
4. Serve over noodles.

Fun Facts

Did you know? Hungarian goulash has been enjoyed since the 9th century and was a favorite among Hungarian shepherds.

6 servings

380 cal

25 min

Spicy Cajun Jambalaya

Experience the bold flavors of the American South in this spicy jambalaya.

Ingredients:

- 1 lb chicken, sliced
- 1 lb andouille sausage, sliced
- 1 bell pepper, diced
- 1 onion, chopped
- 1 cup rice

Directions

1. Sauté chicken, sausage, peppers, and onions.
2. Add rice, spices, and broth.
3. Simmer until rice is tender.
4. Enjoy the heat!

Fun Facts

Did you know? Jambalaya is a Creole dish with Spanish, French, and African influences, making it a true melting pot of flavors.

4
servings

320 cal

20 min

Garlic Butter Mushroom Linguine

Delight in the earthy goodness of garlic butter mushrooms over linguine.

Ingredients:

- 8 oz linguine
- 1 lb mushrooms, sliced
- 4 cloves garlic, minced
- 1/4 cup butter

Directions

1. Cook linguine until al dente.
2. Sauté mushrooms and garlic in butter until tender.
3. Toss with pasta and indulge!

Fun Facts

Did you know? Garlic has been used for centuries for both culinary and medicinal purposes, thanks to its numerous health benefits.

Chapter 3:
Rice & Grain Delights

4
servings

240 cal

20 min

Lemon Herb Rice Pilaf

Elevate your rice with zesty lemon and fragrant herbs.

Ingredients:

- 1 cup long-grain rice
- Zest and juice of 1 lemon
- 2 cups chicken broth
- 2 sprigs fresh thyme

Directions

1. Sauté rice until lightly browned.
2. Add lemon zest, juice, thyme, and broth.
3. Simmer until rice is fluffy.
4. Fluff with a fork and serve.

Fun Facts

Did you know? Pilaf, also known as "pilav" or "pulao," is a versatile dish enjoyed in various forms across the world, from Asia to the Middle East and beyond.

4
servings

310 cal

25 min

Coconut Rice with Black Beans

Transport your taste buds to the tropics with this creamy coconut rice.

Ingredients:

- 1 cup jasmine rice
- 1 cup coconut milk
- 1 can black beans
- 1/2 tsp salt

Directions

1. Rinse rice until water runs clear.
2. Combine rice, coconut milk, salt, and beans.
3. Simmer until rice is tender and coconutty.
4. Enjoy the paradise on a plate!

Fun Facts

Did you know? Coconut rice is a popular side dish in Southeast Asian and Caribbean cuisines, often served with spicy or flavorful main courses.

4 servings

280 cal

20 min

Mediterranean Quinoa

Savor the flavors of the Mediterranean with this vibrant quinoa dish.

Ingredients:

- 1 cup quinoa
- 1/2 cup cherry tomatoes, halved
- 1/2 cup cucumber, diced
- 1/4 cup Kalamata olives
- 2 tbsp olive oil

Directions

1. Rinse quinoa thoroughly.
2. Cook quinoa and fluff with a fork.
3. Toss with tomatoes, cucumber, olives, and olive oil.
4. Relish the Mediterranean magic!

Fun Facts

Did you know? Quinoa is often referred to as a "superfood" due to its high protein content and nutritional value, dating back to its cultivation by the Incas over 3,000 years ago.

4
servings

330 cal

30 min

Teriyaki Rice with Tofu

Enjoy the sweet and savory allure of teriyaki with rice and tofu.

Ingredients:

- 1 cup jasmine rice
- 1/2 cup teriyaki sauce
- 1/2 lb firm tofu, cubed
- 1/2 cup broccoli florets

Directions

1. Rinse rice until water is clear.
2. Cook rice and set aside.
3. Sauté tofu until browned.
4. Add teriyaki sauce and broccoli.
5. Serve over rice and indulge!

Fun Facts

Did you know? Teriyaki sauce is a Japanese cooking technique that involves grilling or broiling foods with a glaze made from soy sauce, sugar, and mirin, resulting in a glossy finish.

4
servings

250 cal

15 min

Lemon Garlic Couscous

Delight in the bright flavors of lemon and garlic in this couscous.

Ingredients:

- 1 cup couscous
- Zest and juice of 1 lemon
- 2 cloves garlic, minced
- 2 tbsp olive oil

Directions

1. Combine couscous, lemon zest, garlic, and olive oil.
2. Pour in lemon juice and hot water.
3. Fluff with a fork.
4. Savor the citrusy delight!

Fun Facts

Did you know? Couscous is a staple food in North African cuisine, often served as a side dish or a base for stews, tagines, and salads.

4
servings

290 cal

25 min

Mexican Rice with Corn

Spice up your meal with this Mexican-inspired rice featuring sweet corn.

Ingredients:

- 1 cup long-grain rice
- 1 cup corn kernels
- 1/2 cup salsa
- 1 tsp cumin
- 1/2 tsp chili powder

Directions

1. Sauté rice until golden.
2. Add corn, salsa, and spices.
3. Simmer until rice is tender and flavorful.
4. Ole! Enjoy your fiesta on a plate.

Fun Facts

Did you know? Mexican rice, often referred to as "arroz rojo," is a popular side dish that's traditionally made with tomatoes, giving it its distinctive red color.

4
servings

270 cal

30 min

Cilantro Lime Farro

A refreshing farro dish bursting with the zing of cilantro and lime.

Ingredients:

- 1 cup farro
- Zest and juice of 2 limes
- 1/2 cup fresh cilantro, chopped
- 2 tbsp olive oil

Directions

1. Cook farro until tender.
2. Mix in lime zest, juice, cilantro, and olive oil.
3. Savor the citrusy herbaceousness!
4. Enjoy as a side or main.

Fun Facts

Did you know? Farro is an ancient grain that was a staple in the diets of ancient Egyptians, Greeks, and Romans, prized for its nutty flavor and nutritional value.

4 servings

350 cal

35 min

Wild Mushroom Risotto

Luxuriate in the earthy, creamy goodness of wild mushroom risotto.

Ingredients:

- 1 cup Arborio rice
- 1/2 lb mixed wild mushrooms, sliced
- 1 onion, minced
- 4 cups vegetable broth

Directions

1. Sauté mushrooms and onions until tender.
2. Add rice and cook until translucent.
3. Gradually add broth and stir until creamy.
4. Experience the risotto perfection!

Fun Facts

Did you know? Risotto is an Italian specialty known for its creamy consistency, achieved through gradual additions of warm broth and constant stirring.

4
servings

260 cal

20 min

Garlic Parmesan Brown Rice

Elevate simple brown rice with the rich flavors of garlic and Parmesan.

Ingredients:

- 1 cup brown rice
- 2 cloves garlic, minced
- 1/4 cup grated Parmesan
- 2 tbsp butter

Directions

1. Cook rice until tender and set aside.
2. Sauté garlic in butter until fragrant.
3. Toss rice with garlic, Parmesan, and salt.
4. Savor the cheesy goodness!

Fun Facts

Did you know? Brown rice is a whole grain that contains more fiber and nutrients than white rice, making it a healthier choice for many dishes.

4
servings

380 cal

25 min

Spicy Sausage and Rice

A bold and hearty combination of spicy sausage and rice.

Ingredients:

- 1 cup long-grain rice
- 1/2 lb spicy sausage, sliced
- 1 bell pepper, diced
- 1 onion, chopped
- 1 can diced tomatoes

Directions

1. Cook rice until fluffy and set aside.
2. Sauté sausage, pepper, and onion until browned.
3. Add tomatoes and simmer.
4. Serve sausage mixture over rice.

Fun Facts

Did you know? Sausages have been enjoyed by various cultures for thousands of years, with countless regional variations in flavor and preparation.

Chapter 4:
Savory Skillets & Stir-Fries

4 servings | 320 cal | 30 min

Teriyaki Chicken Stir-Fry

Dive into the sweet and savory world of teriyaki chicken.

Ingredients:

- 1 lb chicken breasts, sliced
- 1 cup broccoli florets
- 1 bell pepper, sliced
- 1/2 cup teriyaki sauce

Directions

1. Sauté chicken until browned.
2. Add veggies and stir-fry until tender.
3. Pour in teriyaki sauce and heat.
4. Serve over rice and enjoy!

Fun Facts

Did you know? Teriyaki sauce originated in Japan and was traditionally used to glaze fish. It has since become popular worldwide for its sweet and umami flavors.

4 servings **380 cal** **25 min**

Sausage and Vegetable Skillet

A hearty skillet dish featuring sausage and a medley of veggies.

Ingredients:

- 1 lb sausage links, sliced
- 2 cups bell peppers, sliced
- 1 onion, chopped
- 2 cloves garlic, minced

Directions

1. Sauté sausage until browned.
2. Add onions, garlic, and peppers.
3. Cook until veggies are tender.
4. Dive into the deliciousness!

Fun Facts

Did you know? Sausage making has a long history, dating back to ancient civilizations where it was a way to preserve meat before refrigeration.

4
servings

340 cal

30 min

Beef and Broccoli Stir-Fry

Enjoy the classic combination of tender beef and crisp broccoli.

Ingredients:

- 1 lb beef sirloin, sliced
- 2 cups broccoli florets
- 1/2 cup soy sauce
- 2 tbsp brown sugar

Directions

1. Sauté beef until browned and set aside.
2. Stir-fry broccoli until vibrant.
3. Add beef back in and pour soy sauce and sugar.
4. Serve hot.

Fun Facts

Did you know? Beef and broccoli stir-fry is a popular American-Chinese dish, combining the best of both culinary traditions.

4
servings

270 cal

20 min

Lemon Herb Shrimp Skillet

Brighten your day with zesty lemon and succulent shrimp.

Ingredients:

- 1 lb large shrimp, peeled
- Zest and juice of 1 lemon
- 2 cloves garlic, minced
- 2 tbsp fresh parsley

Directions

1. Sauté shrimp until pink and set aside.
2. Sauté garlic and lemon zest.
3. Add shrimp back in with lemon juice and parsley.
4. Savor the citrusy delight!

Fun Facts

Did you know? Shrimp is the most popular seafood in the United States, with the average American consuming over 4 pounds of it per year.

4
servings

260 cal

25 min

Tofu and Snow Pea Stir-Fry

A light and healthy stir-fry featuring tofu and crisp snow peas.

Ingredients:

- 1/2 lb firm tofu, cubed
- 2 cups snow peas
- 2 cloves garlic, minced
- 2 tbsp soy sauce

Directions

1. Sauté tofu until golden and set aside.
2. Stir-fry snow peas and garlic until tender.
3. Add tofu back in with soy sauce.
4. Enjoy the veggie goodness!

Fun Facts

Did you know? Tofu, also known as bean curd, has been a staple in Chinese cuisine for over 2,000 years and is made from soybean milk.

4
servings

380 cal

30 min

Thai Red Curry Chicken

Experience the bold and aromatic flavors of
Thai red curry.

Ingredients:

- 1 lb chicken thighs, sliced
- 1 can coconut milk
- 2 tbsp red curry paste
- 1 cup bell peppers, sliced

Directions

1. Sauté chicken until browned.
2. Add coconut milk and red curry paste.
3. Simmer until chicken is cooked.
4. Stir in bell peppers and serve.

Fun Facts

Did you know? Thai red curry paste is made from
a blend of red chilies, garlic, lemongrass,
galangal, and other aromatic ingredients.

4
servings

330 cal

25 min

Cashew Tofu Stir-Fry

Delight in the crunchy texture of cashews paired with tofu.

Ingredients:

- 1/2 lb firm tofu, cubed
- 1/2 cup cashews
- 2 cups broccoli florets
- 2 tbsp soy sauce

Directions

1. Sauté tofu until golden.
2. Add cashews and stir-fry until lightly browned.
3. Add broccoli and soy sauce.
4. Savor the nutty delight!

Fun Facts

Did you know? Cashews are often referred to as "nature's vitamin pill" due to their rich nutrient content, including vitamins, minerals, and healthy fats.

4
servings

360 cal

30 min

Honey Garlic
Salmon Skillet

Indulge in the sweet and savory combination of honey and garlic.

Ingredients:

- 1 lb salmon fillets
- 2 tbsp honey
- 2 cloves garlic, minced
- 2 tbsp soy sauce

Directions

1. Sauté salmon until browned.
2. Mix honey, garlic, and soy sauce.
3. Pour mixture over salmon and simmer until glazed.
4. Enjoy the salmon perfection!

Fun Facts

Did you know? Salmon is rich in omega-3 fatty acids, which are known for their heart-healthy benefits and can help reduce the risk of cardiovascular disease.

4
servings

350 cal

25 min

Szechuan Beef Stir-Fry

Get ready for a spicy kick with this Szechuan-inspired beef stir-fry.

Ingredients:

- 1 lb beef strips
- 1/4 cup soy sauce
- 2 tbsp Szechuan sauce
- 2 cloves garlic, minced

Directions

1. Sauté beef until browned.
2. Add garlic and stir-fry briefly.
3. Mix in soy sauce and Szechuan sauce.
4. Spice up your meal and enjoy!

Fun Facts

Did you know? Szechuan cuisine is known for its bold and spicy flavors, thanks to the liberal use of Szechuan peppercorns and fiery chili peppers.

4 servings

290 cal

25 min

Mediterranean Chicken and Veggie Skillet

Take a trip to the Mediterranean with this flavorful chicken and veggie skillet.

Ingredients:

- 1 lb chicken breasts, sliced
- 1 cup cherry tomatoes, halved
- 1/2 cup Kalamata olives
- 1/4 cup feta cheese

Directions

1. Sauté chicken until browned.
2. Add tomatoes and olives; cook until heated.
3. Top with feta cheese.
4. Savor the Mediterranean flavors!

Fun Facts

Did you know? The Mediterranean diet is often touted as one of the healthiest diets in the world, known for its emphasis on fresh vegetables, olive oil, and lean proteins.

We have a small favor to ask

Dear Culinary Adventurers and One-Pot Maestros,

Midway through this culinary journey, we want to express our immense gratitude for embarking on this flavor-filled exploration with us. The "One-Pot 5-Ingredient Wonders" cookbook is a testament to the magic that can happen in a single pot, where culinary excellence meets time-efficiency, and delightful aromas fill your kitchen.

We've crafted this collection of recipes with a deep love for simple, yet delicious, cooking. Our hope is that you've already experienced the joy of creating these one-pot marvels and indulged in their fantastic flavors.

Now, we come to you with a small request. In the realm of culinary exploration, reviews are the compass that guide fellow food enthusiasts. Your feedback holds the power to help others discover the culinary wonders found within these pages. Taking a moment to leave a review, assign a star rating, and perhaps share a brief sentence about your journey with the "One-Pot 5-Ingredient Wonders" cookbook could make all the difference.

We genuinely appreciate every review, and we take the time to read and savor each one. Your insights, comments, and suggestions not only help us improve but also assist other home cooks in their gastronomic adventures. By sharing your thoughts, you're fostering a vibrant community of food lovers who appreciate the beauty of simplicity in cooking.

As we return to our culinary voyage, we want to assure you that every recipe is a result of our dedication to perfection. But, like any culinary artist, we are aware that, on rare occasions, a dish might not turn out as expected. We appreciate your understanding if ever there's a culinary hiccup on your journey through these recipes.

With that said, let's return to what brings us all together—our passion for exceptional one-pot creations. As we continue this journey, we hope that each recipe enriches your culinary skills and brings joy to your table.

Once again, thank you for choosing the "One-Pot 5-Ingredient Wonders" cookbook as your culinary companion. We're excited to continue this voyage together, exploring the art of simplified, time-efficient cooking.

To many more one-pot wonders, hearty meals, and shared culinary experiences,

Garden of Grapes

Chapter 5:
Comforting Casseroles

6 servings

420 cal

35 min

Cheesy Baked Ziti

Dive into a world of cheesy delight with this baked ziti.

Ingredients:

- 12 oz ziti pasta
- 2 cups marinara sauce
- 1 1/2 cups shredded mozzarella
- 1/2 cup grated Parmesan

Directions

1. Cook ziti until al dente.
2. Mix pasta with marinara sauce and half of the mozzarella.
3. Transfer to a baking dish and top with remaining mozzarella and Parmesan.
4. Bake until bubbly and golden.
5. Enjoy the gooey goodness!

Fun Facts

Did you know? Baked ziti is a classic Italian-American dish that's often enjoyed at family gatherings and celebrations.

6 servings **380 cal** **40 min**

Chicken and Rice Casserole

A comforting casserole that combines tender chicken and rice.

Ingredients:

- 1 1/2 lbs chicken thighs, boneless
- 1 cup long-grain rice
- 2 cups chicken broth
- 1 cup frozen peas

Directions

1. Season chicken and sear until browned.
2. Remove chicken and sauté rice until translucent.
3. Add chicken back in, pour in chicken broth, and add peas.
4. Bake until chicken is cooked through and rice is tender.
5. Serve and savor the warmth!

Fun Facts

Did you know? Casseroles have been a staple of American home cooking for decades, offering comfort and convenience in one dish.

6 servings

420 cal

45 min

Beef and Potato Casserole

Get cozy with this hearty casserole featuring beef and potatoes.

Ingredients:

- 1 lb ground beef
- 4 cups potatoes, diced
- 1 onion, chopped
- 1 cup cheddar cheese, shredded

Directions

1. Brown ground beef and onion.
2. Layer potatoes in a baking dish and top with beef mixture and cheese.
3. Bake until potatoes are tender and cheese is bubbly.
4. Dig in and relish the comforting flavors!

Fun Facts

Did you know? Casseroles are often associated with comfort food, and their versatility allows for endless variations to suit different tastes.

6
servings

350 cal

30 min

Creamy Tomato Tortellini Bake

Enjoy a creamy and cheesy tortellini bake with tomato goodness.

Ingredients:

- 16 oz cheese tortellini
- 2 cups marinara sauce
- 1/2 cup heavy cream
- 1/2 cup mozzarella cheese

Directions

1. Cook tortellini until al dente.
2. Mix cooked tortellini with marinara sauce and heavy cream.
3. Transfer to a baking dish and sprinkle with mozzarella.
4. Bake until golden and bubbly.
5. Savor the creamy comfort!

Fun Facts

Did you know? Tortellini is a ring-shaped pasta that originated in the Italian region of Emilia-Romagna and is often filled with cheese or meat.

 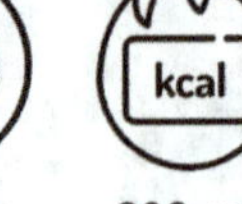 

6
servings

280 cal

35 min

Spinach and Artichoke Dip Casserole

Transform a beloved dip into a delightful casserole experience.

Ingredients:

- 8 oz penne pasta
- 1 cup spinach, chopped
- 1 cup artichoke hearts, chopped
- 1 cup cream cheese

Directions

1. Cook penne pasta until al dente.
2. Combine cooked pasta, spinach, artichoke hearts, and cream cheese in a baking dish.
3. Bake until creamy and bubbly.
4. Dive in with your favorite dippers!
5. Enjoy the dip in a new form!

Fun Facts

Did you know? Spinach and artichoke dip is a popular appetizer that's often served with tortilla chips, crackers, or bread for dipping.

6 servings

320 cal

40 min

Vegan Mexican Casserole

Delight in the flavors of Mexico with this vegan-friendly casserole.

Ingredients:

- 1 cup quinoa
- 1 can black beans, drained
- 1 cup corn kernels
- 1 cup salsa
- 1/2 cup vegan cheese

Directions

1. Cook quinoa until fluffy.
2. Mix quinoa, black beans, corn, and salsa in a baking dish.
3. Sprinkle with vegan cheese.
4. Bake until cheese is melty and bubbly.
5. Savor the vegan fiesta!

Fun Facts

Did you know? Veganism is a lifestyle that avoids the consumption of all animal products, including meat, dairy, and eggs, for ethical, environmental, or health reasons.

6 servings

310 cal

35 min

Tuna Noodle Casserole

Revisit a classic with this comforting tuna noodle casserole.

Ingredients:

- 8 oz egg noodles
- 2 cans tuna, drained
- 1 cup frozen peas
- 1 cup cheddar cheese, shredded
- 1/2 cup mayonnaise

Directions

1. Cook egg noodles until al dente.
2. Mix cooked noodles, tuna, peas, cheddar cheese, and mayonnaise in a baking dish.
3. Bake until bubbly and golden.
4. Dig in and enjoy the nostalgia!

Fun Facts

Did you know? Tuna noodle casserole became popular in the United States during the mid-20th century and has remained a comforting classic ever since.

6
servings

290 cal

40 min

Creamy Broccoli and Rice Bake

Embrace the goodness of broccoli and rice in this creamy bake.

Ingredients:

- 1 1/2 cups white rice
- 2 cups broccoli florets
- 1 cup cheddar cheese, shredded
- 1/2 cup heavy cream

Directions

1. Cook white rice until fluffy.
2. Blanch broccoli until tender.
3. Combine cooked rice, broccoli, cheddar cheese, and heavy cream in a baking dish.
4. Bake until creamy and golden.
5. Savor the creamy comfort!

Fun Facts

Did you know? Broccoli is a member of the cabbage family and is rich in vitamins, minerals, and antioxidants that are beneficial for health.

6 servings **380 cal** **30 min**

Baked Mac and Cheese

Indulge in the ultimate comfort food with this classic mac and cheese.

Ingredients:

- 8 oz elbow macaroni
- 2 cups cheddar cheese, shredded
- 1 cup milk
- 2 tbsp butter
- 2 tbsp flour

Directions

1. Cook macaroni until al dente.
2. Make a roux by melting butter and stirring in flour.
3. Add milk and cheese, stirring until creamy.
4. Combine macaroni and cheese sauce in a baking dish.
5. Bake until bubbly and golden.
6. Dive into the cheesy goodness!

Fun Facts

Did you know? Mac and cheese is a beloved comfort food in the United States, with a rich history dating back to Thomas Jefferson, who popularized macaroni in the early 19th century.

6
servings

330 cal

40 min

Sweet Potato and Black Bean Enchilada Casserole

Spice up your dinner with this flavorful enchilada casserole.

Ingredients:

- 2 sweet potatoes, peeled and diced
- 1 can black beans, drained
- 1 cup enchilada sauce
- 1 cup cheddar cheese, shredded
- 1/4 cup fresh cilantro

Directions

1. Roast sweet potatoes until tender.
2. Mix sweet potatoes, black beans, and enchilada sauce in a baking dish.
3. Top with cheddar cheese.
4. Bake until cheese is melty and bubbly.
5. Garnish with fresh cilantro and enjoy the southwest flavors!

Fun Facts

Did you know? Enchiladas are a traditional Mexican dish made from rolled tortillas filled with various ingredients and topped with a savory sauce.

Chapter 6:
Seafood Suppers

4
servings

300 cal

25 min

Lemon Dill Baked Salmon

Elevate your salmon with the bright flavors of lemon and dill.

Ingredients:

- 4 salmon fillets
- Zest and juice of 1 lemon
- 2 tbsp fresh dill, chopped
- 2 tbsp olive oil

Directions

1. Preheat oven and place salmon on a baking sheet.
2. Drizzle with olive oil, lemon juice, and zest.
3. Sprinkle with dill.
4. Bake until salmon flakes easily.
5. Savor the citrusy delight!

Fun Facts

Did you know? Salmon is a rich source of omega-3 fatty acids, which are essential for brain health and have been linked to numerous health benefits.

4 servings

280 cal

20 min

Garlic Butter Shrimp Scampi

Enjoy succulent shrimp in a garlicky, buttery sauce.

Ingredients:

- 1 lb large shrimp, peeled and deveined
- 4 cloves garlic, minced
- 1/4 cup butter
- 1/4 cup white wine

Directions

1. Sauté garlic in butter until fragrant.
2. Add shrimp and cook until pink.
3. Deglaze with white wine and simmer.
4. Savor the garlic buttery goodness!
5. Serve over pasta or with crusty bread.

Fun Facts

Did you know? Scampi is an Italian-American dish that typically features shrimp or other seafood cooked with garlic, butter, and white wine, often served over pasta.

4
servings

320 cal

25 min

Experience the sweet and savory allure of
teriyaki glazed tuna.

Teriyaki Glazed Tuna Steaks

Ingredients:

- 4 tuna steaks
- 1/2 cup teriyaki sauce
- 2 tbsp brown sugar
- 2 cloves garlic, minced

Directions

1. Mix teriyaki sauce, brown sugar, and garlic.
2. Marinate tuna in the mixture.
3. Grill or sear tuna until desired doneness.
4. Enjoy the teriyaki perfection!
5. Serve with rice and veggies.

Fun Facts

Did you know? Tuna is a popular fish for grilling
and searing due to its meaty texture and mild
flavor, making it a versatile choice for various
cuisines.

4
servings

350 cal

30 min

Coconut Curry Shrimp

Dive into the exotic flavors of coconut curry with succulent shrimp.

Ingredients:

- 1 lb large shrimp, peeled and deveined
- 1 can coconut milk
- 2 tbsp red curry paste
- 1 cup bell peppers, sliced

Directions

1. Sauté shrimp until pink and set aside.
2. Simmer coconut milk and curry paste.
3. Add bell peppers and cooked shrimp.
4. Savor the creamy curry!
5. Serve with rice.

Fun Facts

Did you know? Coconut curry is a popular dish in Southeast Asian cuisines, known for its rich, aromatic flavors and creamy coconut milk base.

4
servings

290 cal

20 min

Spice up your meal with blackened catfish fillets.

Blackened Catfish Fillets

Ingredients:

- 4 catfish fillets
- 2 tbsp blackening seasoning
- 2 tbsp olive oil

Directions

1. Coat catfish fillets with blackening seasoning.
2. Heat olive oil in a skillet.
3. Sear catfish on both sides until blackened and cooked through.
4. Savor the spicy, smoky flavor!
5. Serve with coleslaw or rice.

Fun Facts

Did you know? Blackening is a cooking technique that involves coating fish or other proteins with a spicy seasoning mix and then cooking it in a hot skillet, creating a flavorful crust.

4
servings

380 cal

35 min

Creamy Garlic Butter Lobster Tails

Indulge in the luxurious flavor of lobster tails with garlic butter.

Ingredients:

- 4 lobster tails
- 4 cloves garlic, minced
- 1/2 cup butter
- 1/4 cup fresh parsley, chopped

Directions

1. Preheat oven and prepare lobster tails.
2. Combine garlic, butter, and parsley.
3. Brush mixture over lobster tails.
4. Bake until lobster is opaque and tender.
5. Savor the decadent delight!
6. Serve with lemon wedges.

Fun Facts

Did you know? Lobster is often considered a delicacy and is enjoyed in various dishes, from lobster bisque to lobster rolls, for its sweet and tender meat.

4 servings

320 cal

30 min

Spicy Cajun Crawfish Boil

Spice things up with a Cajun crawfish boil featuring corn and potatoes.

Ingredients:

- 2 lbs crawfish
- 4 corn cobs, halved
- 4 potatoes, quartered
- 2 tbsp Cajun seasoning
- 2 tbsp butter

Directions

1. Bring a large pot of water to a boil and add Cajun seasoning and butter.
2. Add potatoes and corn; cook until tender.
3. Add crawfish and cook until bright red.
4. Drain and serve the spicy Cajun goodness!
5. Enjoy with dipping sauces.

Fun Facts

Did you know? Crawfish boils are a popular tradition in Louisiana, especially during the spring and early summer, when crawfish are in season and plentiful.

4
servings

280 cal

25 min

Tomato Basil Cod

Delight in the freshness of tomato and basil with tender cod.

Ingredients:

- 4 cod fillets
- 2 cups cherry tomatoes, halved
- 1/2 cup fresh basil, chopped
- 2 cloves garlic, minced

Directions

1. Sauté garlic until fragrant and set aside.
2. Season cod fillets with salt and pepper.
3. Cook cod until opaque.
4. Add cherry tomatoes and basil; cook briefly.
5. Savor the tomato basil goodness!
6. Serve with a drizzle of olive oil.

Fun Facts

Did you know? Cod is a popular fish for its mild flavor and versatility in various cuisines, from traditional fish and chips to Mediterranean-inspired dishes.

4
servings

310 cal

30 min

Citrus Grilled Swordfish

Enjoy the zing of citrus-marinated swordfish on the grill.

Ingredients:

- 4 swordfish steaks
- Zest and juice of 1 lemon
- Zest and juice of 1 orange
- 2 cloves garlic, minced

Directions

1. Combine citrus zest, juice, and garlic in a bowl.
2. Marinate swordfish in the mixture.
3. Grill swordfish until cooked through and lightly charred.
4. Savor the citrusy grilled goodness!
5. Serve with a side of grilled vegetables.

Fun Facts

Did you know? Swordfish is a firm and meaty fish that's often grilled or seared to bring out its natural flavors and textures.

4
servings

290 cal

25 min

Shrimp and Broccoli Stir-Fry

Dive into a quick and healthy stir-fry featuring shrimp and broccoli.

Ingredients:

- 1 lb large shrimp, peeled and deveined
- 4 cups broccoli florets
- 2 cloves garlic, minced
- 1/4 cup soy sauce

Directions

1. Sauté garlic until fragrant.
2. Add shrimp and cook until pink; set aside.
3. Stir-fry broccoli until tender.
4. Return shrimp to the pan and add soy sauce.
5. Savor the shrimp and broccoli harmony!
6. Serve over rice.

Fun Facts

Did you know? Stir-frying is a cooking technique that originated in China and involves quick cooking over high heat, preserving the color, texture, and nutrients of the ingredients.

Chapter 7:
Vegetarian Vibes

4
servings

240 cal

40 min

Spinach and Feta Stuffed Peppers

Elevate bell peppers with a filling of spinach and creamy feta.

Ingredients:

- 4 bell peppers
- 2 cups fresh spinach
- 1 cup crumbled feta
- 1 cup cooked rice
- 2 tbsp olive oil

Directions

1. Preheat oven and prepare bell peppers.
2. Sauté spinach until wilted; mix with cooked rice and feta.
3. Stuff peppers with the mixture.
4. Bake until peppers are tender.
5. Savor the cheesy goodness!
6. Serve with a drizzle of olive oil.

Fun Facts

Did you know? Bell peppers come in various colors, including green, red, yellow, and orange, and each color has a slightly different flavor and sweetness level.

4
servings

180 cal

20 min

Garlic Butter Mushrooms with Spinach

Enjoy the earthy flavors of garlic butter mushrooms and spinach.

Ingredients:

- 1 lb mushrooms, sliced
- 4 cups fresh spinach
- 4 cloves garlic, minced
- 1/4 cup butter
- Salt and pepper to taste

Directions

1. Sauté mushrooms until browned and set aside.
2. In the same pan, melt butter and add garlic.
3. Add spinach and cook until wilted.
4. Return mushrooms to the pan and mix.
5. Savor the garlic butter delight!
6. Season with salt and pepper.

Fun Facts

Did you know? Mushrooms are a unique food source because they are one of the few natural sources of vitamin D, which is essential for bone health and overall well-being.

4
servings

320 cal

30 min

Sweet Potato and Chickpea Curry

Dive into the warm and comforting flavors of sweet potato curry.

Ingredients:

- 2 sweet potatoes, peeled and diced
- 1 can chickpeas, drained
- 1 can coconut milk
- 2 tbsp curry powder
- 1 cup fresh cilantro

Directions

1. Sauté sweet potatoes until tender.
2. Add chickpeas and curry powder; cook briefly.
3. Pour in coconut milk and simmer.
4. Garnish with fresh cilantro.
5. Savor the curry goodness!
6. Serve with rice or naan.

Fun Facts

Did you know? Curry is a broad term used to describe a variety of spiced dishes, and it varies in flavor and heat level depending on the type of spices used.

4
servings

220 cal

20 min

Caprese Zucchini Noodles

Enjoy a fresh twist on the classic Caprese salad with zucchini noodles.

Ingredients:

- 4 zucchinis, spiralized
- 2 cups cherry tomatoes, halved
- 1 cup fresh mozzarella, diced
- 1/4 cup fresh basil, chopped
- 2 tbsp balsamic glaze

Directions

1. Spiralize zucchinis into noodles and set aside.
2. Combine zucchini noodles, cherry tomatoes, mozzarella, and basil.
3. Drizzle with balsamic glaze.
4. Savor the Caprese freshness!
5. Season with salt and pepper.

Fun Facts

Did you know? Caprese salad is a classic Italian dish that showcases the colors of the Italian flag with its combination of red tomatoes, green basil, and white mozzarella.

4 servings

280 cal

30 min

Vegan Spinach Artichoke Pasta

Indulge in a creamy spinach artichoke pasta without dairy.

Ingredients:

- 8 oz pasta of your choice
- 2 cups fresh spinach
- 1 can artichoke hearts, drained and chopped
- 1 cup unsweetened almond milk
- 2 tbsp nutritional yeast

Directions

1. Cook pasta until al dente and set aside.
2. Sauté spinach until wilted; add artichoke hearts.
3. Pour in almond milk and nutritional yeast; simmer until creamy.
4. Combine pasta and sauce.
5. Savor the vegan indulgence!
6. Season with salt and pepper.

Fun Facts

Did you know? Nutritional yeast is a popular ingredient in vegan cooking, known for its cheesy flavor and the wealth of vitamins and minerals it provides.

4
servings

320 cal

40 min

Vegetarian Chili

Warm up with a hearty and flavorful vegetarian chili.

Ingredients:

- 2 cans kidney beans, drained
- 1 can diced tomatoes
- 1 cup corn kernels
- 1 onion, chopped
- 2 cloves garlic, minced
- 2 tbsp chili powder

Directions

1. Sauté onions and garlic until fragrant.
2. Add kidney beans, diced tomatoes, corn, and chili powder; simmer until flavors meld.
3. Savor the chili warmth!
4. Serve with your favorite toppings.
5. Season with salt and pepper.

Fun Facts

Did you know? Chili is a popular American dish with a rich history, and there are countless regional variations, from Texas chili with no beans to Cincinnati chili served over spaghetti.

4
servings

310 cal

35 min

Creamy Mushroom Risotto

Delight in the creamy richness of mushroom risotto.

Ingredients:

- 1 1/2 cups Arborio rice
- 8 oz mushrooms, sliced
- 2 cloves garlic, minced
- 1/2 cup white wine
- 4 cups vegetable broth

Directions

1. Sauté mushrooms and garlic until browned and set aside.
2. Toast Arborio rice until translucent.
3. Deglaze with white wine; cook until absorbed.
4. Gradually add vegetable broth, stirring until creamy.
5. Return mushrooms to the risotto.
6. Savor the creamy delight!
7. Season with salt and pepper.

Fun Facts

Did you know? Arborio rice is a short-grain rice that is often used in Italian risotto dishes due to its ability to absorb liquid and create a creamy texture.

4 servings

280 cal

45 min

Mediterranean Stuffed Bell Peppers

Embark on a Mediterranean journey with stuffed bell peppers.

Ingredients:

- 4 bell peppers
- 1 cup cooked quinoa
- 1 cup chickpeas, drained
- 1 cup cherry tomatoes, halved
- 1/2 cup feta cheese, crumbled
- 2 tbsp olive oil

Directions

1. Preheat oven and prepare bell peppers.
2. Mix quinoa, chickpeas, cherry tomatoes, and feta cheese.
3. Stuff peppers with the mixture.
4. Bake until peppers are tender.
5. Savor the Mediterranean flavors!
6. Drizzle with olive oil.

Fun Facts

Did you know? The Mediterranean diet is often considered one of the healthiest diets in the world, known for its emphasis on fresh vegetables, olive oil, and lean proteins.

4
servings

250 cal

20 min

Lemon Herb Quinoa Salad

Enjoy the freshness of lemon and herbs in a quinoa salad.

Ingredients:

- 1 cup quinoa
- Zest and juice of 1 lemon
- 2 tbsp fresh herbs (e.g., parsley, mint, or cilantro), chopped
- 1/4 cup olive oil
- Salt and pepper to taste

Directions

1. Cook quinoa until fluffy and set aside.
2. Combine quinoa, lemon zest, lemon juice, and fresh herbs.
3. Drizzle with olive oil.
4. Savor the zesty herbiness!
5. Season with salt and pepper.
6. Serve chilled.

Fun Facts

Did you know? Quinoa is a nutritious grain that is high in protein and contains all nine essential amino acids, making it a complete protein source.

4
servings

280 cal

25 min

Beet and Goat Cheese Salad

Elevate your salad with the vibrant colors of beets and creamy goat cheese.

Ingredients:

- 4 cups mixed greens
- 2 beets, roasted and sliced
- 1/2 cup goat cheese, crumbled
- 1/4 cup balsamic vinaigrette
- 1/4 cup walnuts, toasted

Directions

1. Roast and slice beets and set aside.
2. Toss mixed greens with balsamic vinaigrette.
3. Top with roasted beets, goat cheese, and toasted walnuts.
4. Savor the beet and goat cheese harmony!
5. Season with salt and pepper.

Fun Facts

Did you know? Beets are rich in antioxidants and have been associated with various health benefits, including improved cardiovascular health and enhanced exercise performance.

Chapter 8:
International Inspirations

4
servings

340 cal

40 min

Chicken Tikka Masala

Savor the flavors of India with creamy chicken tikka masala.

Ingredients:

- 1 lb chicken breasts, diced
- 1 cup tomato sauce
- 1/2 cup heavy cream
- 2 tbsp garam masala
- 2 tbsp vegetable oil

Directions

1. Sauté diced chicken in vegetable oil until browned; set aside.
2. In the same pan, add garam masala and tomato sauce; simmer.
3. Pour in heavy cream and return chicken to the pan.
4. Savor the creamy Indian delight!
5. Serve with rice or naan.

Fun Facts

Did you know? Chicken tikka masala is a popular British dish with origins in India. It consists of marinated and grilled chicken served in a creamy tomato-based sauce.

4
servings

380 cal

60 min

Beef Pho

Experience the aromatic flavors of Vietnamese beef pho.

Ingredients:

- 1 lb beef sirloin, thinly sliced
- 8 cups beef broth
- 8 oz rice noodles
- 2 star anise
- 2 cinnamon sticks

Directions

1. In a large pot, simmer beef broth with star anise and cinnamon sticks for 30 minutes.
2. Cook rice noodles according to package instructions.
3. Divide cooked noodles among serving bowls and top with beef slices.
4. Pour hot broth over the beef to cook it.
5. Savor the fragrant Vietnamese pho!
6. Serve with fresh herbs and lime wedges.

Fun Facts

Did you know? Pho is a traditional Vietnamese soup that is typically made with beef or chicken and flavored with aromatic spices and herbs. It's a beloved street food in Vietnam and worldwide.

4
servings

320 cal

30 min

Vegan Thai Green Curry

Enjoy the vibrant flavors of Thailand with vegan green curry.

Ingredients:

- 2 cups mixed vegetables (e.g., bell peppers, broccoli, and carrots)
- 1 can coconut milk
- 2 tbsp green curry paste
- 2 tbsp soy sauce
- 2 cups cooked rice

Directions

1. Sauté mixed vegetables until tender.
2. Add green curry paste and soy sauce; stir.
3. Pour in coconut milk and simmer.
4. Savor the vegan Thai delight!
5. Serve over cooked rice.
6. Garnish with fresh herbs.

Fun Facts

Did you know? Thai green curry is known for its fragrant green chili paste and creamy coconut milk, creating a balance of spiciness and creaminess in each bite.

4
servings

380 cal

45 min

Shrimp and Sausage Gumbo

Dive into the flavors of the American South with shrimp and sausage gumbo.

Ingredients:

- 1 lb shrimp, peeled and deveined
- 8 oz Andouille sausage, sliced
- 1 cup bell peppers, chopped
- 1 cup okra, sliced
- 1/4 cup roux (store-bought or homemade)

Directions

1. Sauté Andouille sausage until browned; set aside.
2. In the same pot, add bell peppers and okra; cook until tender.
3. Stir in roux and simmer.
4. Add shrimp and cooked sausage; simmer until shrimp turn pink.
5. Savor the hearty Louisiana gumbo!
6. Serve with rice.

Fun Facts

Did you know? Gumbo is a popular dish in Louisiana, with a rich history influenced by French, African, and Spanish cuisines. It's known for its thick, flavorful roux-based sauce and diverse ingredients.

4
servings

300 cal

35 min

Moroccan Chickpea Tagine

Embark on a culinary journey to Morocco with chickpea tagine.

Ingredients:

- 2 cans chickpeas, drained
- 2 cups diced tomatoes
- 2 tbsp Moroccan spice blend (Ras el Hanout)
- 1/2 cup dried apricots, chopped
- 1/4 cup fresh cilantro, chopped

Directions

1. Combine chickpeas, diced tomatoes, Moroccan spice blend, and dried apricots in a tagine or large pot.
2. Simmer until flavors meld.
3. Savor the Moroccan tagine!
4. Garnish with fresh cilantro.
5. Serve with couscous.

Fun Facts

Did you know? Tagine refers to both the Moroccan dish and the special pot it's cooked in. The tagine pot has a unique conical lid that allows steam to circulate, ensuring even cooking.

4
servings

320 cal

40 min

Tandoori Chicken

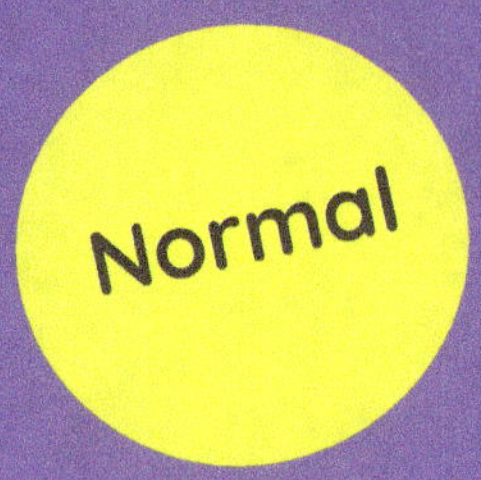

Indulge in the bold flavors of India with tandoori chicken.

Ingredients:

- 1 lb chicken thighs, boneless
- 1/2 cup plain yogurt
- 2 tbsp tandoori spice blend
- 2 tbsp lemon juice
- 2 tbsp vegetable oil

Directions

1. Marinate chicken in yogurt, tandoori spice blend, lemon juice, and vegetable oil for at least 30 minutes.
2. Grill or roast until chicken is cooked through and slightly charred.
3. Savor the smoky tandoori delight!
4. Serve with naan and yogurt sauce.

Fun Facts

Did you know? Tandoori chicken gets its name from the tandoor, a traditional clay oven used in Indian cooking. The intense heat of the tandoor imparts a unique smoky flavor to the dish.

4
servings

340 cal

35 min

Spicy Korean Bulgogi

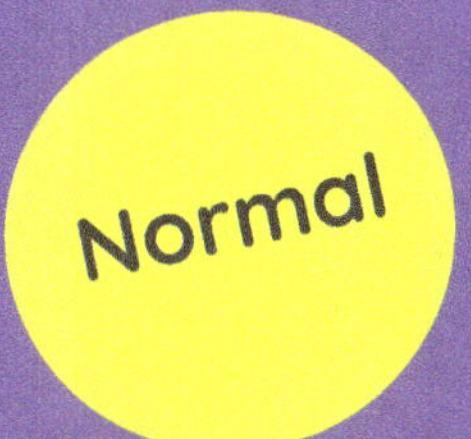

Spice up your meal with the fiery flavors of Korean bulgogi.

Ingredients:

- 1 lb beef sirloin, thinly sliced
- 1/4 cup soy sauce
- 2 tbsp sugar
- 2 tbsp gochujang (Korean red chili paste)
- 4 cloves garlic, minced

Directions

1. Marinate beef in soy sauce, sugar, gochujang, and minced garlic for at least 30 minutes.
2. Sauté beef until cooked through and slightly caramelized.
3. Savor the spicy Korean delight!
4. Serve with rice and pickled vegetables.

Fun Facts

Did you know? Bulgogi is a popular Korean dish made from thinly sliced marinated beef that is grilled or stir-fried. The marinade typically includes soy sauce, sugar, garlic, and various seasonings.

4
servings

280 cal

30 min

Vegetable Pad Thai

Enjoy the sweet and savory flavors of Thailand with vegetable pad Thai.

Ingredients:

- 8 oz rice noodles
- 2 cups mixed vegetables (e.g., bell peppers, carrots, and broccoli)
- 1/4 cup soy sauce
- 2 tbsp brown sugar
- 2 tbsp lime juice

Directions

1. Cook rice noodles until al dente; set aside.
2. Sauté mixed vegetables until tender.
3. In a separate bowl, combine soy sauce, brown sugar, and lime juice.
4. Toss cooked noodles and sauce with vegetables.
5. Savor the Thai noodle goodness!
6. Garnish with chopped peanuts and fresh cilantro.

Fun Facts

Did you know? Pad Thai is one of Thailand's most famous dishes, known for its balance of sweet, sour, salty, and spicy flavors. It's often garnished with crushed peanuts and fresh herbs.

4
servings

350 cal

30 min

Italian Sausage and Peppers

Experience the flavors of Italy with Italian sausage and peppers.

Ingredients:

- 4 Italian sausages
- 2 bell peppers, sliced
- 1 onion, sliced
- 1 can crushed tomatoes
- 2 cloves garlic, minced

Directions

1. Sauté Italian sausages until browned; set aside.
2. In the same pan, sauté bell peppers and onions until tender.
3. Add crushed tomatoes and minced garlic; simmer.
4. Return sausages to the pan and cook until heated through.
5. Savor the Italian comfort!
6. Serve with crusty bread or over pasta.

Fun Facts

Did you know? Sausage and peppers is a classic Italian-American dish often served at festivals and street fairs. It's known for its hearty and savory flavors.

4
servings

340 cal

45 min

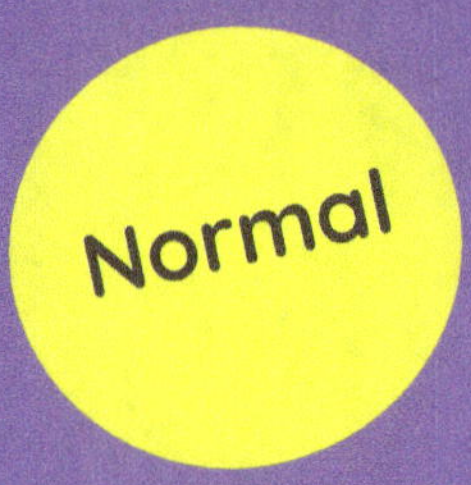

Brazilian Feijoada

Dive into the flavors of Brazil with hearty feijoada.

Ingredients:

- 1 lb black beans, cooked
- 8 oz pork sausage, sliced
- 8 oz smoked sausage, sliced
- 1/2 lb pork shoulder, diced
- 2 cloves garlic, minced
- 2 bay leaves

Directions

1. In a large pot, sauté garlic until fragrant.
2. Add pork shoulder and sauté until browned.
3. Stir in cooked black beans, pork sausage, smoked sausage, and bay leaves.
4. Simmer until flavors meld.
5. Savor the Brazilian feijoada!
6. Serve with rice and orange slices.

Fun Facts

Did you know? Feijoada is Brazil's national dish, known for its rich and hearty combination of black beans and various pork cuts. It's traditionally served with rice, collard greens, and orange slices.

Chapter 9:
Breakfast & Brunch Delights

4
servings

320 cal

30 min

One-Pot Breakfast Skillet

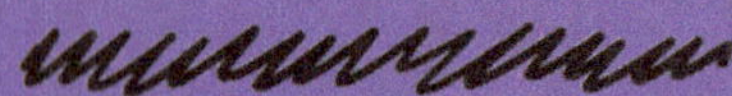

Start your day right with a hearty one-pot breakfast skillet.

Ingredients:

- 4 eggs
- 4 strips bacon, chopped
- 2 cups frozen hash browns
- 1 cup shredded cheddar cheese
- Salt and pepper to taste

Directions

1. In a large skillet, cook chopped bacon until crispy; set aside.
2. Add frozen hash browns to the skillet and cook until crispy.
3. Create wells in the hash browns and crack eggs into them.
4. Sprinkle with cooked bacon and cheddar cheese.
5. Cover and cook until eggs are set.
6. Savor the skillet breakfast!
7. Season with salt and pepper.

Fun Facts

Did you know? One-pot breakfast skillets are a versatile dish that allows you to customize ingredients based on your preferences, making it a perfect breakfast solution for busy mornings.

4
servings

280 cal

35 min

Vegetarian Breakfast Hash

Enjoy a meatless morning with this flavorful vegetarian breakfast hash.

Ingredients:

- 2 cups diced potatoes
- 1 cup diced bell peppers
- 1 cup diced onions
- 1 cup diced tomatoes
- 4 eggs

Directions

1. In a large skillet, sauté diced potatoes until browned and crispy.
2. Add diced bell peppers and onions; cook until tender.
3. Stir in diced tomatoes and create wells in the hash.
4. Crack eggs into the wells and cover until eggs are set.
5. Savor the vegetarian hash!
6. Season with salt and pepper.

Fun Facts

Did you know? Breakfast hashes are a great way to use up leftover vegetables and ingredients from your fridge, making them a sustainable and delicious choice.

4 servings

350 cal

45 min

Mexican Breakfast Casserole

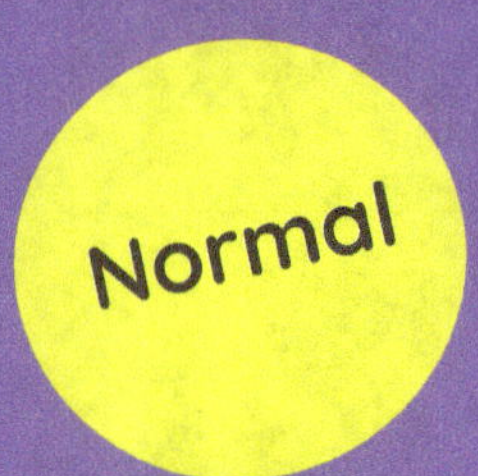

Spice up your morning with a savory Mexican breakfast casserole.

Ingredients:

- 6 eggs
- 1 cup black beans, drained
- 1 cup diced tomatoes
- 1 cup diced bell peppers
- 1 cup shredded cheddar cheese
- 1 tsp chili powder

Directions

1. In a baking dish, whisk eggs and chili powder.
2. Stir in black beans, diced tomatoes, and diced bell peppers.
3. Top with shredded cheddar cheese.
4. Bake until eggs are set and cheese is melted.
5. Savor the Mexican flavors!
6. Garnish with fresh cilantro if desired.

Fun Facts

Did you know? Mexican breakfast casseroles are a popular choice for brunch gatherings and can be prepared in advance, making them a convenient option for hosting.

Cinnamon Roll Oatmeal

Satisfy your sweet tooth with creamy cinnamon roll oatmeal.

Ingredients:

- 2 cups rolled oats
- 4 cups milk of your choice
- 1/4 cup brown sugar
- 1 tsp ground cinnamon
- 1/4 cup cream cheese icing (store-bought or homemade)

Directions

1. In a saucepan, combine rolled oats, milk, brown sugar, and ground cinnamon.
2. Simmer until oats are cooked and mixture is creamy.
3. Drizzle with cream cheese icing.
4. Savor the cinnamon roll oatmeal!
5. Garnish with extra cinnamon if desired.

Fun Facts

Did you know? Cinnamon roll oatmeal captures the classic flavors of a cinnamon roll in a comforting and wholesome breakfast dish, perfect for chilly mornings.

4
servings

320 cal

40 min

Hash Brown Breakfast Bake

Dive into the cheesy goodness of a hash brown breakfast bake.

Ingredients:

- 2 cups frozen hash browns
- 1 cup diced ham
- 1 cup diced bell peppers
- 1 cup shredded cheddar cheese
- 4 eggs

Directions

1. In a baking dish, layer frozen hash browns, diced ham, and diced bell peppers.
2. Sprinkle with shredded cheddar cheese.
3. Create wells in the mixture and crack eggs into them.
4. Bake until eggs are set and hash browns are crispy.
5. Savor the cheesy breakfast bake!
6. Season with salt and pepper.

Fun Facts

Did you know? Hash brown breakfast bakes are a crowd-pleaser and can be customized with your favorite breakfast ingredients, making them a versatile choice for brunch.

4
servings

300 cal

30 min

Quinoa Breakfast Bowl

Fuel your morning with a nutritious quinoa breakfast bowl.

Ingredients:

- 2 cups cooked quinoa
- 1 cup Greek yogurt
- 1 cup mixed berries
- 1/4 cup honey
- 1/4 cup chopped nuts (e.g., almonds or walnuts)

Directions

1. In serving bowls, layer cooked quinoa, Greek yogurt, and mixed berries.
2. Drizzle with honey and sprinkle with chopped nuts.
3. Savor the quinoa breakfast bowl!
4. Customize with additional toppings if desired.

Fun Facts

Did you know? Quinoa is a nutrient-rich grain that is high in protein, fiber, and essential vitamins and minerals, making it an excellent choice for a satisfying breakfast.

4
servings

320 cal

35 min

One-Pot Frittata

Whip up a fuss-free one-pot frittata for a delightful breakfast.

Ingredients:

- 6 eggs
- 1 cup diced ham
- 1 cup diced bell peppers
- 1 cup diced onions
- 1 cup shredded cheddar cheese

Directions

1. In a large skillet, sauté diced ham, bell peppers, and onions until tender.
2. Whisk eggs and pour them over the sautéed ingredients.
3. Sprinkle with shredded cheddar cheese.
4. Cover and cook until eggs are set.
5. Savor the one-pot frittata!
6. Season with salt and pepper.

Fun Facts

Did you know? Frittatas are a versatile dish that allows you to use up leftover ingredients from your fridge, making them a creative and sustainable breakfast option.

4
servings

280 cal

25 min

Vegan Breakfast Tacos

Start your day with plant-based goodness in vegan breakfast tacos.

Ingredients:

- 8 small corn tortillas
- 1 cup tofu, crumbled
- 1 cup black beans, drained
- 1 cup diced tomatoes
- 1/4 cup fresh cilantro, chopped
- 1/4 cup avocado, sliced

Directions

1. Warm corn tortillas in a skillet or microwave.
2. Sauté crumbled tofu until heated through.
3. Assemble tacos with tofu, black beans, diced tomatoes, fresh cilantro, and sliced avocado.
4. Savor the vegan breakfast tacos!
5. Drizzle with your favorite vegan sauce if desired.

Fun Facts

Did you know? Vegan breakfast tacos are a delicious and cruelty-free alternative to traditional breakfast tacos, offering a burst of flavors and textures.

4
servings

360 cal

40 min

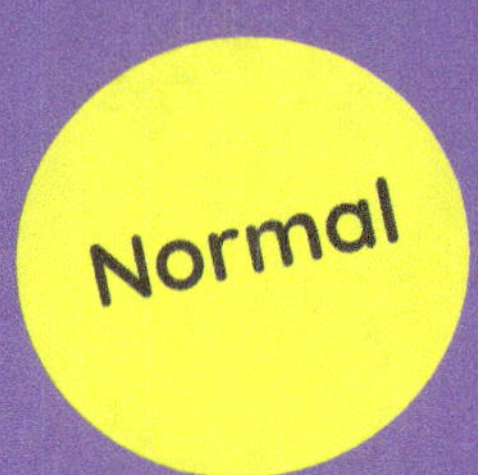

Strawberry
Pancake Cobbler

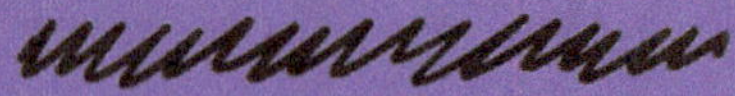

Indulge in the sweet delight of strawberry
pancake cobbler.

Ingredients:

- 2 cups pancake mix
- 1 cup milk
- 2 cups sliced strawberries
- 1/4 cup granulated sugar
- 1/4 cup maple syrup

Directions

1. In a bowl, mix pancake mix and milk until combined.
2. In a baking dish, layer sliced strawberries and sprinkle with granulated sugar.
3. Pour pancake batter over strawberries.
4. Bake until golden and bubbly.
5. Savor the pancake cobbler!
6. Drizzle with maple syrup.

Fun Facts

Did you know? Strawberry pancake cobbler combines the best of both worlds by merging the comfort of pancakes with the sweetness of strawberry cobbler, creating a delightful breakfast treat.

4
servings

340 cal

45 min

Blueberry French Toast Bake

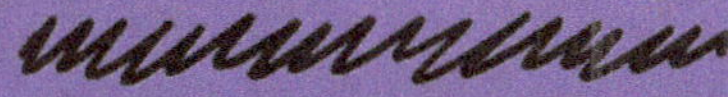

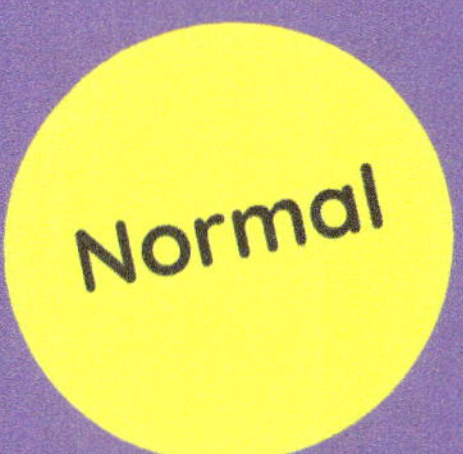

Delight in the classic flavors of blueberry French toast bake.

Ingredients:

- 8 slices bread, cubed
- 1 cup blueberries
- 4 eggs
- 1 cup milk
- 1/4 cup maple syrup

Directions

1. In a baking dish, layer cubed bread and blueberries.
2. In a bowl, whisk eggs, milk, and maple syrup.
3. Pour egg mixture over the bread and blueberries.
4. Bake until golden and set.
5. Savor the French toast bake!
6. Drizzle with extra maple syrup if desired.

Fun Facts

Did you know? French toast bakes are a convenient way to enjoy the flavors of classic French toast without the hassle of individual dipping and frying.

Chapter 10:
Dessert Delights

4 servings

320 cal

15 min

One-Pot Chocolate Fondue

Dive into a world of sweetness with one-pot chocolate fondue.

Ingredients:

- 8 oz dark chocolate, chopped
- 1 cup heavy cream
- 1 tsp vanilla extract
- Assorted dippers (e.g., strawberries, marshmallows, and pretzels)

Directions

1. In a saucepan, heat heavy cream until it simmers.
2. Remove from heat and add chopped dark chocolate and vanilla extract.
3. Stir until smooth and creamy.
4. Transfer to a fondue pot or serving dish.
5. Dip and savor the chocolatey delight!
6. Enjoy with assorted dippers.

Fun Facts

Did you know? Chocolate fondue is a popular dessert that originated in Switzerland. It's all about dipping bite-sized treats into melted chocolate for a delightful experience.

4 servings

300 cal

40 min

Apple Crisp

Warm your heart with a comforting apple crisp dessert.

Ingredients:

- 4 cups sliced apples (e.g., Granny Smith or Honeycrisp)
- 1 cup rolled oats
- 1/2 cup brown sugar
- 1/4 cup butter, melted
- 1 tsp ground cinnamon

Directions

1. In a baking dish, layer sliced apples.
2. In a bowl, mix rolled oats, brown sugar, melted butter, and ground cinnamon.
3. Sprinkle oat mixture over the apples.
4. Bake until golden and bubbling.
5. Savor the apple crisp!
6. Serve with vanilla ice cream if desired.

Fun Facts

Did you know? Apple crisp is a beloved dessert that combines the sweetness of baked apples with a crunchy oat and sugar topping. It's often served warm with a scoop of ice cream.

4 servings **280 cal** **20 min**

Rice Krispies Treats

Relive your childhood with the classic Rice Krispies Treats.

Ingredients:

- 4 cups Rice Krispies cereal
- 1/4 cup butter
- 1 package (10 oz) marshmallows
- 1/2 tsp vanilla extract

Directions

1. In a large pot, melt butter over low heat.
2. Add marshmallows and stir until completely melted.
3. Remove from heat and stir in vanilla extract.
4. Fold in Rice Krispies cereal until well coated.
5. Press mixture into a greased pan.
6. Let cool and cut into squares.
7. Savor the crispy nostalgia!

Fun Facts

Did you know? Rice Krispies Treats were invented in 1939 by Malitta Jensen and popularized by Kellogg's in the 1940s. They are known for their simplicity and deliciousness.

4
servings

340 cal

30 min

Chocolate Peanut Butter Fudge

Satisfy your sweet tooth with creamy chocolate peanut butter fudge.

Ingredients:

- 1 cup semi-sweet chocolate chips
- 1 cup creamy peanut butter
- 1/2 cup sweetened condensed milk
- 1 tsp vanilla extract
- A pinch of salt

Directions

1. In a microwave-safe bowl, combine semi-sweet chocolate chips and peanut butter.
2. Microwave in 30-second intervals, stirring until smooth.
3. Stir in sweetened condensed milk, vanilla extract, and a pinch of salt.
4. Pour mixture into a greased pan and refrigerate until set.
5. Cut into squares.
6. Savor the chocolatey peanut butter fudge!
7. Store in the refrigerator.

Fun Facts

Did you know? Fudge has a long history and is believed to have originated in the late 19th century in the United States. It's known for its rich, dense, and sweet flavor.

4
servings

280 cal

40 min

Coconut Tapioca Pudding

Experience the tropical flavors of coconut tapioca pudding.

Ingredients:

- 1/2 cup small pearl tapioca
- 2 cups coconut milk
- 1/4 cup sugar
- 1/4 tsp salt
- 1/2 tsp vanilla extract

Directions

1. Soak tapioca pearls in water for 30 minutes, then drain.
2. In a saucepan, combine soaked tapioca, coconut milk, sugar, salt, and vanilla extract.
3. Bring to a simmer and cook until tapioca is translucent and mixture is thick.
4. Remove from heat and let cool.
5. Savor the creamy coconut tapioca pudding!
6. Chill before serving.

Fun Facts

Did you know? Tapioca pudding is made from tapioca pearls, which are derived from the cassava plant. It's known for its unique texture and can be enjoyed in various flavors, including coconut.

4
servings

320 cal

45 min

Cherry Cobbler

Indulge in the sweet and fruity goodness of cherry cobbler.

Ingredients:

- 2 cups canned cherries, drained
- 1/2 cup granulated sugar
- 1 cup all-purpose flour
- 1/4 cup butter, melted
- 1/2 cup milk

Directions

1. In a baking dish, layer canned cherries and sprinkle with granulated sugar.
2. In a bowl, mix all-purpose flour, melted butter, and milk until smooth.
3. Pour batter over the cherries.
4. Bake until golden and bubbling.
5. Savor the cherry cobbler!
6. Serve with vanilla ice cream if desired.

Fun Facts

Did you know? Cobbler is a dessert of British origin that features a fruit filling topped with a batter, biscuit, or dough crust. It's often served warm and is a comforting treat.

4
servings

280 cal

35 min

Brighten your day with the tangy goodness of lemon bars.

Lemon Bars

Ingredients:

- 1 cup all-purpose flour
- 1/2 cup unsalted butter, softened
- 1/4 cup powdered sugar
- 2 large eggs
- 1 cup granulated sugar
- 2 tbsp lemon juice

Directions

1. In a bowl, mix all-purpose flour, softened unsalted butter, and powdered sugar until crumbly.
2. Press mixture into a greased pan and bake until lightly golden.
3. In another bowl, whisk together eggs, granulated sugar, and lemon juice.
4. Pour lemon mixture over the baked crust.
5. Bake until set and lightly browned.
6. Savor the tangy lemon bars!
7. Dust with powdered sugar before serving.

Fun Facts

Did you know? Lemon bars are a classic dessert that combines a buttery crust with a zesty lemon filling. They are a delightful balance of sweet and tangy flavors.

4 servings

340 cal

20 min

S'mores Dip

Bring the campfire experience home with delectable s'mores dip.

Ingredients:

- 1 cup milk chocolate chips
- 1 cup marshmallows
- Graham crackers for dipping

Directions

1. Preheat your oven's broiler.
2. In an oven-safe dish, layer milk chocolate chips.
3. Top with marshmallows.
4. Place under the broiler for 1-2 minutes or until marshmallows are toasted.
5. Savor the gooey s'mores dip!
6. Serve with graham crackers for dipping.

Fun Facts

Did you know? S'mores are a beloved outdoor treat traditionally made by roasting marshmallows over a campfire and sandwiching them with chocolate between graham crackers.

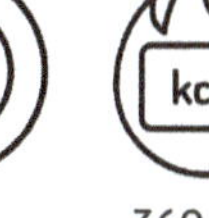

4 servings   **360 cal**   **30 min**

Strawberry Shortcake Skillet

Enjoy a classic dessert with a twist - strawberry shortcake skillet.

Ingredients:

- 2 cups strawberries, sliced
- 1/4 cup granulated sugar
- 1 cup all-purpose flour
- 2 tbsp granulated sugar
- 1/2 tsp baking powder
- 1/4 tsp baking soda
- 1/4 cup unsalted butter, cold and cubed
- 1/2 cup buttermilk

Directions

1. In a bowl, combine sliced strawberries and 1/4 cup granulated sugar.
2. In another bowl, mix all-purpose flour, 2 tbsp granulated sugar, baking powder, and baking soda.
3. Cut in cold, cubed unsalted butter until the mixture resembles coarse crumbs.
4. Stir in buttermilk to form a dough.
5. Transfer dough to a greased skillet and bake until golden.
6. Serve strawberry shortcake warm with macerated strawberries on top.
7. Savor the fruity delight!

Fun Facts

Did you know? Strawberry shortcake is a beloved dessert that originated in the United States. It typically consists of a sweet biscuit or cake topped with fresh strawberries and whipped cream.

4 servings

320 cal

20 min

Peanut Butter Chocolate Rice Krispies

Satisfy your cravings with the perfect blend of peanut butter and chocolate in Rice Krispies form.

Ingredients:

- 4 cups Rice Krispies cereal
- 1/2 cup creamy peanut butter
- 1 cup milk chocolate chips
- 1/4 cup butter
- 1/2 cup powdered sugar

Directions

1. In a large pot, melt butter over low heat.
2. Add peanut butter and milk chocolate chips; stir until smooth.
3. Remove from heat and fold in Rice Krispies cereal.
4. Press mixture into a greased pan.
5. In a separate bowl, sift powdered sugar over the top.
6. Savor the peanut butter chocolate goodness!
7. Let cool and cut into squares.

Fun Facts

Did you know? Peanut butter chocolate Rice Krispies treats combine the creamy richness of peanut butter with the sweetness of milk chocolate for an irresistible dessert.

Chapter 11:
Quick & Easy Sides

4
servings

120 cal

25 min

Garlic Parmesan Roasted Broccoli

Easy

Elevate your meal with the savory goodness of roasted broccoli.

Ingredients:

- 1 lb broccoli florets
- 2 tbsp olive oil
- 2 cloves garlic, minced
- 1/4 cup grated Parmesan cheese

Directions

1. Preheat your oven to 425°F (220°C).
2. In a bowl, toss broccoli florets with olive oil and minced garlic.
3. Spread the broccoli on a baking sheet in a single layer.
4. Roast for 20 minutes or until tender and slightly crispy.
5. Sprinkle with grated Parmesan cheese.
6. Savor the garlic Parmesan roasted broccoli!
7. Serve immediately.

Fun Facts

Did you know? Roasting broccoli enhances its flavor and texture, making it a delicious and nutritious side dish that pairs well with various main courses.

4
servings

100 cal

20 min

Lemon Butter Asparagus

Brighten your plate with lemon butter asparagus.

Ingredients:

- 1 lb asparagus spears
- 2 tbsp butter
- 1 tbsp lemon juice
- Zest of 1 lemon
- Salt and pepper to taste

Directions

1. Trim the tough ends of the asparagus spears.
2. In a skillet, melt butter over medium-high heat.
3. Add asparagus and sauté until tender-crisp, about 5 minutes.
4. Drizzle with lemon juice and sprinkle with lemon zest.
5. Savor the lemon butter asparagus!
6. Season with salt and pepper.

Fun Facts

Did you know? Asparagus is a nutrient-rich vegetable that is known for its distinctive flavor and versatility in cooking. It pairs wonderfully with citrusy flavors like lemon.

4 servings

140 cal

25 min

Balsamic Glazed Brussels Sprouts

Enjoy the sweet and tangy goodness of balsamic glazed Brussels sprouts.

Ingredients:

- 1 lb Brussels sprouts, trimmed and halved
- 2 tbsp olive oil
- 2 tbsp balsamic vinegar
- 1 tbsp honey
- Salt and pepper to taste

Directions

1. Preheat your oven to 400°F (200°C).
2. In a bowl, toss Brussels sprouts with olive oil, balsamic vinegar, and honey.
3. Spread them on a baking sheet in a single layer.
4. Roast for 20 minutes or until tender and caramelized.
5. Savor the balsamic glazed Brussels sprouts!
6. Season with salt and pepper.

Fun Facts

Did you know? Balsamic glazed Brussels sprouts are a delightful combination of caramelized sweetness from honey and tanginess from balsamic vinegar. They make a wonderful side dish for special occasions.

4 servings | **120 cal** | **20 min**

Honey Glazed Carrots

Add a touch of sweetness to your meal with honey glazed carrots.

Ingredients:

- 1 lb carrots, peeled and sliced
- 2 tbsp butter
- 2 tbsp honey
- Salt and pepper to taste

Directions

1. In a skillet, melt butter over medium heat.
2. Add sliced carrots and sauté until they start to brown, about 5 minutes.
3. Drizzle with honey and continue to cook until carrots are tender, about 10 minutes.
4. Savor the honey glazed carrots!
5. Season with salt and pepper.

Fun Facts

Did you know? Honey glazed carrots are a classic side dish that pairs well with a wide range of main courses. The honey adds a delightful sweetness to the carrots.

4
servings

250 cal

30 min

Garlic Mashed Potatoes

Embrace the creamy comfort of garlic mashed potatoes.

Ingredients:

- 4 large russet potatoes, peeled and diced
- 4 cloves garlic, minced
- 1/4 cup butter
- 1/2 cup milk
- Salt and pepper to taste

Directions

1. Place diced potatoes and minced garlic in a large pot and cover with cold water.
2. Bring to a boil and simmer until potatoes are fork-tender, about 15 minutes.
3. Drain the potatoes and return them to the pot.
4. Add butter and milk, then mash until smooth and creamy.
5. Savor the garlic mashed potatoes!
6. Season with salt and pepper.

Fun Facts

Did you know? Garlic mashed potatoes are a beloved side dish that combines the creamy goodness of mashed potatoes with the savory flavor of garlic. They are a comfort food staple.

4
servings

150 cal

25 min

Creamed Spinach

Dive into the creamy indulgence of creamed spinach.

Ingredients:

- 1 lb fresh spinach
- 2 tbsp butter
- 2 cloves garlic, minced
- 1/4 cup heavy cream
- 1/4 cup grated Parmesan cheese
- Salt and pepper to taste

Directions

1. In a skillet, melt butter over medium heat.
2. Add minced garlic and sauté until fragrant, about 1 minute.
3. Add fresh spinach and cook until wilted.
4. Stir in heavy cream and grated Parmesan cheese.
5. Savor the creamy spinach!
6. Season with salt and pepper.

Fun Facts

Did you know? Creamed spinach is a classic side dish that combines the earthy flavors of spinach with the richness of heavy cream and Parmesan cheese. It's a perfect accompaniment to steak or chicken.

4 servings · **120 cal** · **30 min**

Roasted Garlic Cauliflower

Enjoy the nutty flavor of roasted garlic cauliflower.

Ingredients:

- 1 head cauliflower, cut into florets
- 2 tbsp olive oil
- 4 cloves garlic, minced
- Salt and pepper to taste

Directions

1. Preheat your oven to 425°F (220°C).
2. In a bowl, toss cauliflower florets with olive oil and minced garlic.
3. Spread the cauliflower on a baking sheet in a single layer.
4. Roast for 25 minutes or until tender and golden.
5. Savor the roasted garlic cauliflower!
6. Season with salt and pepper.

Fun Facts

Did you know? Roasted garlic cauliflower is a flavorful and healthy side dish that offers a unique twist on traditional cauliflower. It's perfect for garlic lovers.

4 servings **180 cal** **20 min**

Mexican Street Corn

Add a burst of flavor to your meal with Mexican street corn.

Ingredients:

- 4 ears corn, husked
- 1/4 cup mayonnaise
- 1/4 cup sour cream
- 1/2 cup crumbled cotija cheese
- 1 tsp chili powder
- Fresh cilantro and lime wedges for garnish

Directions

1. Grill or boil corn until cooked and slightly charred.
2. Mix mayonnaise and sour cream in a bowl.
3. Spread the mixture over each ear of corn.
4. Sprinkle with crumbled cotija cheese and chili powder.
5. Garnish with fresh cilantro and serve with lime wedges.
6. Savor the Mexican street corn!

Fun Facts

Did you know? Mexican street corn, also known as "elote," is a popular street food in Mexico. It's known for its creamy, cheesy, and slightly spicy flavor profile.

4
servings

280 cal

30 min

Mediterranean Couscous Salad

Transport your taste buds to the Mediterranean with couscous salad.

Ingredients:

- 1 cup couscous
- 1 1/4 cups vegetable broth
- 1 cup cherry tomatoes, halved
- 1/2 cucumber, diced
- 1/4 cup Kalamata olives, pitted and sliced
- 1/4 cup feta cheese, crumbled
- 2 tbsp olive oil
- 2 tbsp fresh lemon juice
- Fresh parsley for garnish
- Salt and pepper to taste

Directions

1. In a saucepan, bring vegetable broth to a boil.
2. Stir in couscous, cover, and remove from heat.
3. Let stand for 5 minutes, then fluff with a fork.
4. In a bowl, combine cooked couscous, cherry tomatoes, cucumber, Kalamata olives, and feta cheese.
5. Drizzle with olive oil and fresh lemon juice.
6. Garnish with fresh parsley.
7. Savor the Mediterranean couscous salad!
8. Season with salt and pepper.

Fun Facts

Did you know? Mediterranean couscous salad is a refreshing and wholesome side dish that combines the flavors of the Mediterranean region, featuring ingredients like olives, feta cheese, and fresh lemon juice.

4
servings

220 cal

20 min

Cilantro Lime Rice

Elevate your meal with the zesty goodness of cilantro lime rice.

Ingredients:

- 1 cup long-grain white rice
- 2 cups water
- Zest and juice of 2 limes
- 1/4 cup fresh cilantro, chopped
- Salt to taste

Directions

1. In a saucepan, combine rice and water.
2. Bring to a boil, then reduce heat to low, cover, and simmer for 15-20 minutes or until rice is cooked and water is absorbed.
3. Fluff the cooked rice with a fork.
4. Stir in lime zest, lime juice, and fresh cilantro.
5. Savor the cilantro lime rice!
6. Season with salt to taste.

Fun Facts

Did you know? Cilantro lime rice is a popular side dish in Mexican and Tex-Mex cuisine. It adds a burst of fresh flavor to your meal and pairs perfectly with dishes like burritos and tacos.

We have a small favor to ask

Dear One-Pot Maestros and Culinary Adventurers,

As we wrap up this culinary journey through the "One-Pot 5-Ingredient Wonders" cookbook, we can't help but reflect on the incredible voyage we've embarked upon together. It's been a testament to the simplicity and beauty of one-pot cooking, and your support and enthusiasm have made it all the more meaningful.

Our aim with this book was to offer you a repertoire of easy, time-efficient recipes that let you create culinary excellence with minimal effort. We sincerely hope that these simplified dishes have brought joy to your tables, delighted your taste buds, and eased the burden of everyday cooking.

Your trust in our recipes has been the secret ingredient that has flavored this entire experience. You, the readers, have turned these basic ingredients into extraordinary creations. The "One-Pot 5-Ingredient Wonders" cookbook has become a part of your culinary repertoire, and we're profoundly grateful for that.

Now, here comes a small favor we'd like to ask of you. Reviews are like the finishing touch to a well-prepared dish – they make it truly complete. If you could spare a moment to leave a review, assign a star rating, and perhaps share a brief sentence or two about your journey through this cookbook, you would be contributing not just to us but to the wider community of home cooks.

Each review is a vital ingredient to us, and we read and appreciate every single one. Your insights, feedback, and suggestions are invaluable in helping us shape our future endeavors in simplifying your cooking experience.

In our pursuit of culinary excellence, we aim to make every recipe perfect. Yet, the kitchen is a place where, just like in life, even the best of us can encounter an occasional hiccup. We hope that your reviews are a reflection of our commitment to providing you with the best one-pot recipes and that you kindly understand if we ever fall short.

As we bring this chapter to a close, we want to express our heartfelt gratitude for choosing the "One-Pot 5-Ingredient Wonders" cookbook as your guide through the world of simplified cooking. Your support, your culinary creations, and your connection to our recipes mean the world to us. You've made our dishes a part of your life, and for that, we're immensely thankful.

We eagerly anticipate being a part of more of your culinary adventures and continuing to be your trusted source for simplified cooking delights. Your experiences guide us, and we are profoundly grateful for your ongoing support.

With genuine appreciation and a shared love for one-pot wonders,
Garden of Grapes